Little Jimmy

This story was adapted from *Philippines: The Land That I Love*
Written Dr. Jeannie Hoffman

By DOLORES D. BURNS

Illustrated by SOCRATES BARTOLO

Edited by MARY PENNINGTON

ANEKO
PRESS

"I am going home!" announced little five-year-old Jimmy McElroy.

Surprised, his mother Betty responded, "But you are home!"

"No, Mommy, I'm not Jimmy McElroy anymore." Jimmy pretended, "I'm Jimmy Hale and I am going home."

Little Jimmy McElroy packed his suitcase. Mrs. McElroy was not worried. Their good friends, the Hales, lived across the yard, and Jimmy visited them often.

With his little suitcase in hand,
Jimmy crossed the wooden bridge
to Mr. and Mrs. Hale's house.

He opened the Hale's backdoor and strolled into their kitchen to find Mrs. Hale making soup.

Jimmy announced, "I am Jimmy Hale."

Mrs. Hale smiled and decided to play along with Jimmy's game thinking that he would go home that evening.

Jimmy enjoyed helping Mr. Hale to do small chores. The Hales had decided to paint their house. Little Jimmy thought he was the supervisor as he instructed Mr. Hale to paint the house red. Mr. Hale thought pink would be a nicer color.

Jimmy also loved helping Mrs. Hale bake chocolate chip cookies, which were little Jimmy's favorite. Mrs. Hale did most of the baking and little Jimmy did most of the eating.

When evening came, Mrs. Hale reminded little Jimmy, "It's time to go home now, Jimmy."

"No, Ma'am, I <u>am</u> home. I am sleeping here," little Jimmy insisted politely.

In response, Mrs. Hale said, "Okay, then you have to sleep in the boys' room."

Mrs. Hale phoned Mrs. McElroy to make sure it was okay with her.

Little Jimmy stayed with the Hales for almost a week. Occasionally, he visited his family and even ate supper with them, but after eating, he would walk back to the Hale's house to sleep.

Little Jimmy's mother missed him more and more each day. She decided that it was time for Jimmy to come home, but she had to come up with a plan to make him want to come home on his own.

"Ice Cream!" she thought. Ice Cream was not always available in that part of the Philippines so getting some was an extra special treat. She quickly phoned Mrs. Hale with her idea.

The following day, Little Jimmy's mother walked to the Hale's house. Mrs. Hale let her in with a knowing nod.

"We are going out for an ice cream treat after dinner tonight!" Mrs. McElroy announced with a loud voice so everyone in the house could hear. "We would like to invite little Jimmy Hale to go with us."

To that, Mrs. Hale replied with a wink, "I am sorry but little Jimmy <u>Hale</u> has chores to do. He can't go."

As soon as little Jimmy heard the words ice cream, he suddenly realized that <u>he</u> was Jimmy McElroy, not Jimmy Hale! He hurriedly packed his little suitcase and grabbed his mother's hand to take her home.

"I am Jimmy McElroy," little Jimmy thought.

Never again did little Jimmy think that he was anyone else but Jimmy McElroy.

Spot on the six differences!

Jimmy McElroy - Hale - McElroy
By Velma Hale as told to Leonora Castillo

immy McElroy was the only son of Barton and Betty McElroy, missionaries in the hilippines. They lived next door to Mr. and Mrs. James Willis and Velma Hale, also issionaries to the Philippines.

immy was supervising the building of the Hales' house, or so he thought. And he nstructed Mr. Hale to paint the house red. Mr. Hale thought pink was better. We ainted it white and brown.

Jimmy really liked helping Mr. Hale with any work and helping Mrs. Hale with any chocolate chip cookies, he was about five years old. One day he packed his bag, told his Mother his name was Jimmy Hale and that he was going home. So across the yard he went with his little suitcase. Imagine Mrs. Hale's surprise when Jimmy made this announcement in her kitchen. She went along with him, as she thought that when it was bedtime he would want to go home. Jimmy politely told Mrs. Hale that he lived with them now and he was home. So at bedtime, Mrs. Hale told Jimmy that he could sleep with the boys, Leonardo and Constancio, as they were living with the Hales at this time.

Jimmy stayed about a week, calling himself Jimmy Hale and doing little chores around the house with Mr. Hale and the boys. He occasionally would visit the McElroys, even staying for supper once in a while. His Mother, Betty, decided it was time for him to come home and cooked up a little scheme. The McElroy family was going to the Port Area for ice cream, a very special treat, and invited Jimmy Hale to go along. But Mrs. Hale said that Jimmy could not go because he had work to do. Almost immediately, Jimmy remembered that his name was Jimmy McElroy.

Jim McElroy Age Five